HOW MY BODY **WORKS**
Breathing

Anita Ganeri

Evans

Evans Brothers Limited

First published by Evans Brothers Limited in 2006
2a Portman Mansions
Chiltern St
London W1U 6NR

British Library Cataloguing in Publication Data
Ganeri, Anita
Take a deep breath.
  1. Respiration - Juvenile literature
  2. Human physiology - Juvenile literature
  I. Title
612.2

ISBN 0 237 53184 4
13-digit ISBN (from 1 January 2007) 978 0 237 53184 3

Credits

Editorial: Louise John
Design: Mark Holt & Big Blu Design
Artworks: Julian Baker
Consultant: Dr M Turner
Photographs: Steve Shott
Production: Jenny Mulvanny

Printed in China by WKT Co. Ltd

Acknowledgements
The author and publisher would like to thank the following for kind permission to reproduce photographs:

Science Photo Library, p.15 (CNRI), p.17 (Professors P. Motta/Department of Anatomy/University 'La Sapienza', Rome), p.20 (NASA), p.23 (Professors Motta, Correr and Nottola/University 'La Sapienza', Rome), p.26 (David M Martin, MD).

Models from Truly Scrumptious Ltd. With thanks to: Frankie Iszard, Oliver Hood, Jade Hardie, Ben Ifrah, Diandra Beckles, Arron Henry, Sophie Raven. Copyright © Evans Brothers Ltd 2003.

VISIT OUR WEBSITE
www.evansbooks.co.uk

Contents

How do you breathe?

We all need to breathe air to stay alive. When you breathe in, you pull fresh air into your body. Fresh air is something your body cannot do without, even for a few minutes. This is because air has an important gas called **oxygen** in it. When you breathe, oxygen travels all around your body. Your body needs oxygen to make it work.

The parts of your body you use for breathing are called your **respiratory system**. You can see the different parts of the respiratory system in this picture.

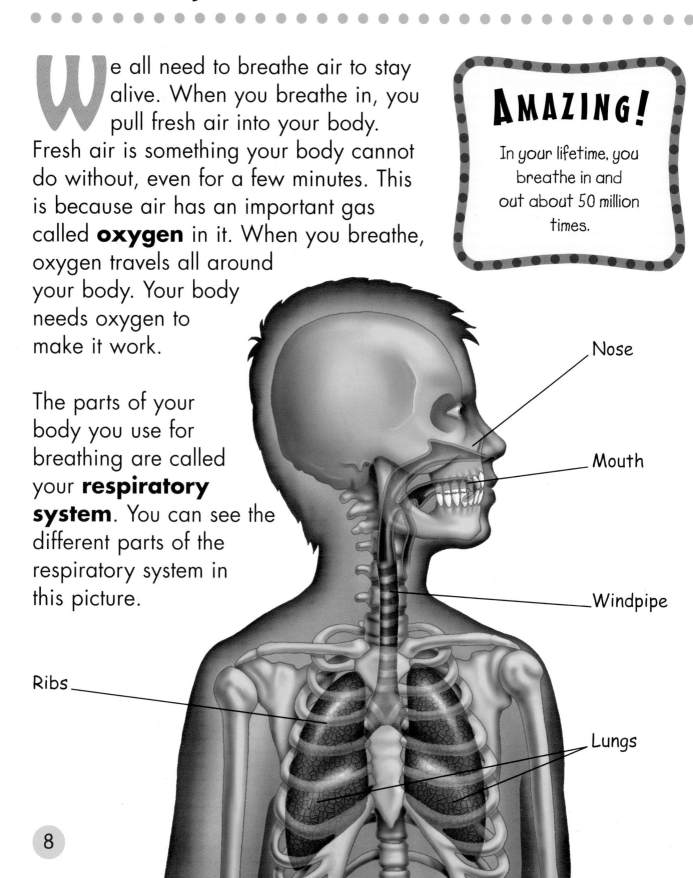

Nose

Mouth

Windpipe

Ribs

Lungs

8

You probably take breathing for granted. This is because it happens automatically. Your amazing brain controls your breathing so that you do it all the time. Most of the time, you don't even think about taking a breath.

LOOK AT ME! LOOK AT ME! LOOK AT ME! LOOK AT ME! LOOK AT ME! LOOK AT ME!

How many goes does it take you to blow out all the candles on your birthday cake? Can you do it in one go? Take a deep breath, then blow.

Breathe in...

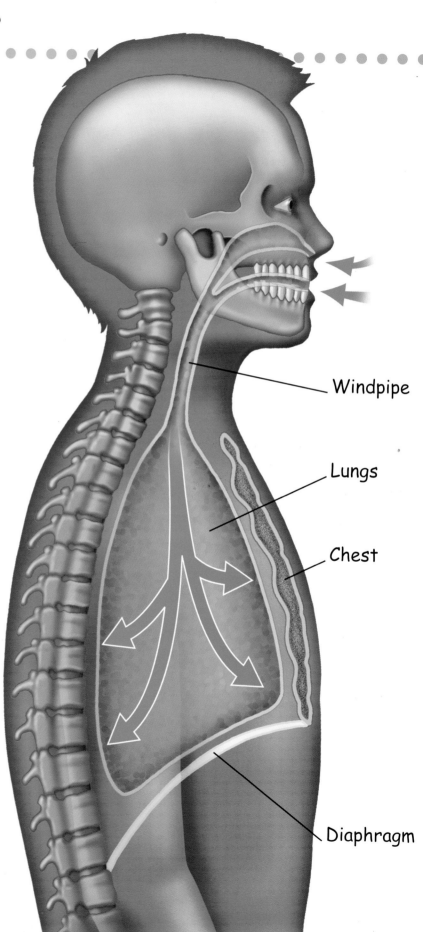

ake a deep breath. When you breathe in, you take in air through your mouth or nose. Then the air goes down a large air tube in your throat, called your windpipe. Inside your **chest**, your windpipe splits into two smaller tubes. Then these tubes split into even smaller tubes which lead into your two lungs. These tubes look a bit like tiny branches on a tree.

AMAZING!

Your windpipe is about 10 cm long. That's about half the length of a drinking straw.

Windpipe

Lungs

Chest

Diaphragm

When you breathe in, your chest gets bigger so that your lungs have room to fill up with air. To do this, your ribs move up and out. A special flat muscle under your lungs moves downwards. This muscle is called your **diaphragm**.

Do you ever get hiccups? This happens if your diaphragm muscle twitches sharply as you breathe in. You take a sudden gasp of breath and make a 'HIC' sound! To stop too much air rushing in, a flap at the top of your windpipe snaps shut. This makes the 'CUP' sound. HICCUP!

LOOK AT ME!

Fold your arms across your chest and breathe in. Can you feel your chest getting bigger as your lungs fill up with air?

Breathe out...

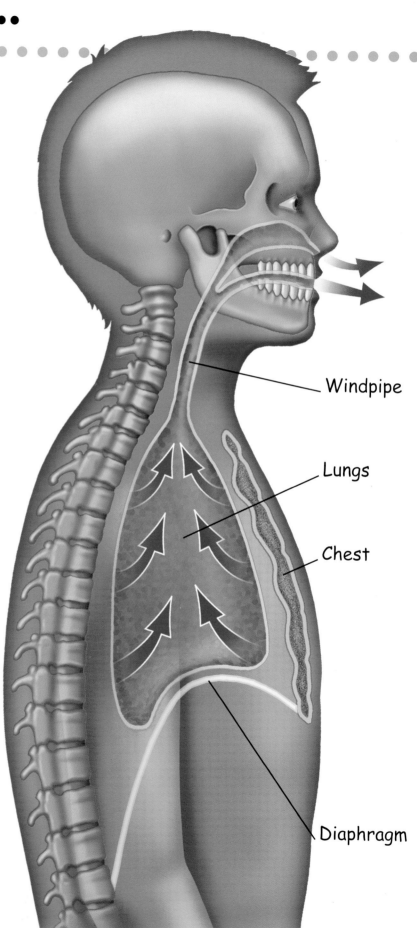

When you breathe out, your ribs move down to squeeze air out of your lungs. Your diaphragm muscle moves upwards. The air goes up through the tubes in your chest and up through your windpipe. Then you blow the air out through your mouth or nose.

Windpipe

Lungs

Chest

Diaphragm

LOOK AT ME!

How loudly can you whistle? When you whistle, you use the air flowing out of your lungs to make a high sound. See if you can whistle a song.

When you breathe out, you push stale air out of your lungs. Stale air has a gas called **carbon dioxide** in it. If you do not breathe this old air out, it can harm your body.

You can't usually see the air you breathe out except on a cold day. Then it looks like white, wispy puffs of steam. These puffs are made of tiny drops of water in your breath.

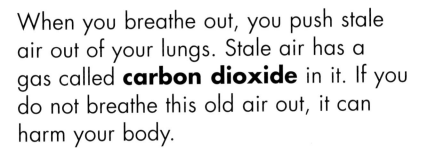

AMAZING!

When you blow up a party balloon, you are filling it with old, stale air!

Your lungs

Your lungs are like two big spongy bags inside your chest that hold air. Your two lungs are not quite the same size. Your left lung is slightly smaller than your right lung, to make enough room in your chest for your heart.

Tiny air tubes lead into your lungs. At the ends of these tubes are tiny bubbles which are called **alveoli**. When you breathe in, the alveoli fill up with air.

LOOK AT ME! LOOK AT ME! LOOK AT ME! LOOK AT ME!

Look at the shape of a bunch of grapes. The tiny alveoli in your lungs look a bit like this.

14

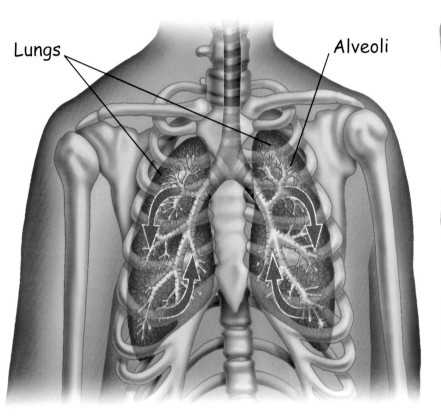

Lungs

Alveoli

AMAZING!

If you could spread the alveoli in your lungs out flat, they would cover a space the size of a tennis court!

Oxygen from the air seeps through the alveoli into your blood and it is carried all around your body. Then, carbon dioxide gas passes from your blood back into the bubbles to be breathed out.

Each of your lungs has about 300 million alveoli. Each air bubble is about the size of a pinhead. They give your lungs a very big surface for soaking up lots of oxygen.

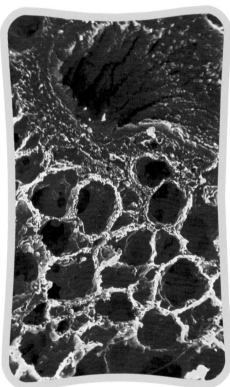

This is what your alveoli look like under a microscope.

Red blood

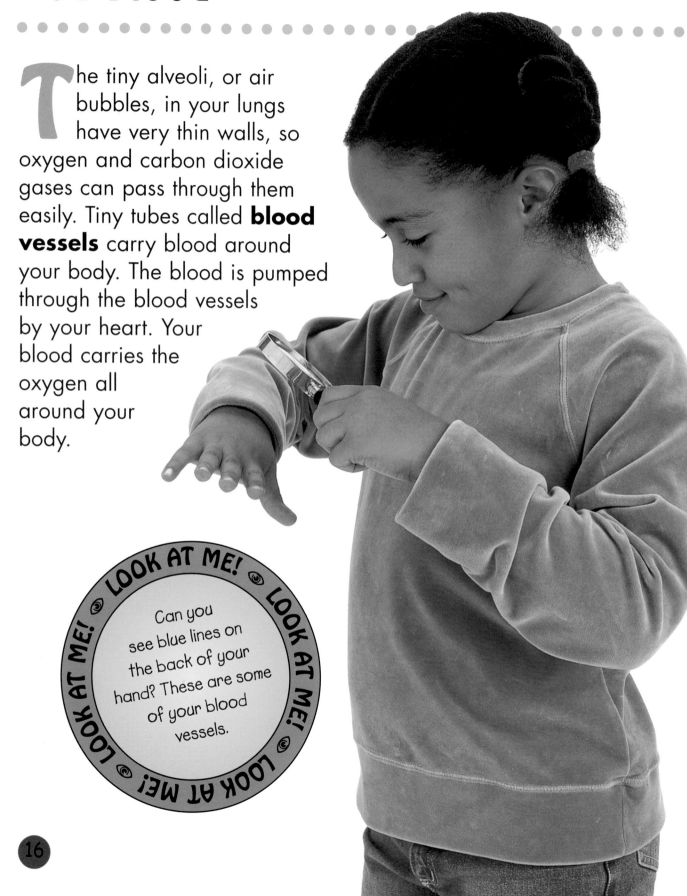

The tiny alveoli, or air bubbles, in your lungs have very thin walls, so oxygen and carbon dioxide gases can pass through them easily. Tiny tubes called **blood vessels** carry blood around your body. The blood is pumped through the blood vessels by your heart. Your blood carries the oxygen all around your body.

LOOK AT ME! ◉ LOOK AT ME! ◉ LOOK AT ME! ◉ LOOK AT ME! ◉

Can you see blue lines on the back of your hand? These are some of your blood vessels.

16

A special chemical in your blood soaks the oxygen up. This chemical makes your blood look red. When the oxygen is used up, your blood turns purply-blue. The oxygen helps to give you **energy**.

Your blood also collects carbon dioxide gas from your body. This is a waste that your body makes. Your blood carries the carbon dioxide back to your lungs and then you breathe it out.

Bone marrow shown under a microscope.

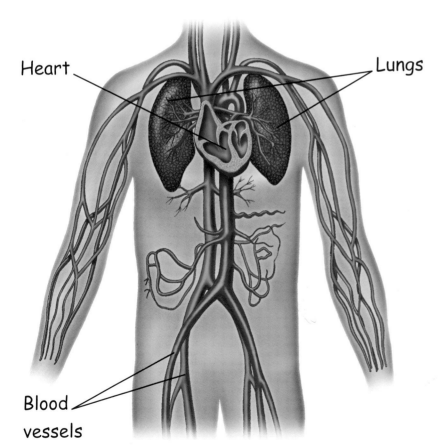

Heart

Lungs

Blood vessels

Enough air?

You need to breathe all the time. Otherwise your body would die. But you do not have to think about breathing, you do it automatically. If you hold your breath for too long, your brain makes you breathe again.

The number of times you breathe in and out depends on your age. You need to breathe about 30 times a minute, whilst an adult needs to breathe about 15 times a minute.

AMAZING!

In a day, you breathe enough air to fill about 500 party balloons.

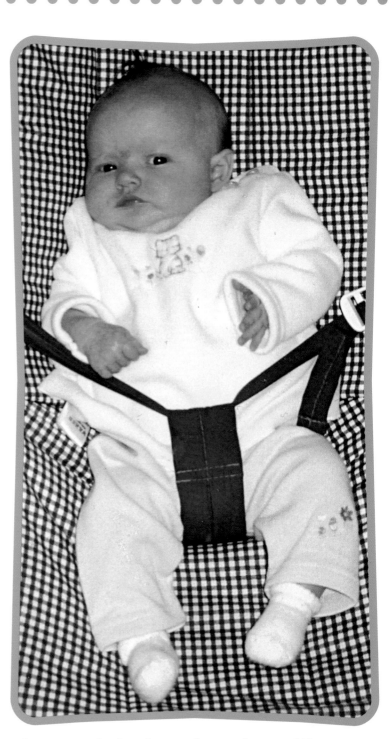

A young baby breathes about 40 times a minute.

The amount of air you need to breathe depends on what you are doing. In a normal breath, you take in about a cupful of air. But if you are running, you take in about ten times that much. This is because your busy body needs more oxygen to give it more energy. When you're asleep, your body needs less oxygen. So your breaths are slower and shallower than when you are awake.

LOOK AT ME! LOOK AT ME! LOOK AT ME! LOOK AT ME!

Do you feel puffed when you've been running? That's because your body needs extra air to replace all the oxygen you've used up.

High up and deep down

Whatever you do, you need to breathe air to stay alive. But sometimes there is very little air or no air at all. Mountaineers often take extra oxygen to breathe when they are climbing high up. This is because the higher up a mountain you go, the less oxygen there is for you to breathe.

Some people live high up in the mountains all year round. You would find it hard to breathe but they are used to it. Their red blood cells are better at trapping oxygen than yours, so they can breathe more easily.

An astronaut on the moon.

AMAZING!

Like people, hardy mountain animals, such as llamas and yaks, are able to trap more oxygen in their blood so that they can breathe.

In space there is no air to breathe. The astronauts who landed on the moon had an oxygen supply on their backs in a tank. It supplied oxygen into their helmets.

There is no air at all to breathe underwater, so deep-sea divers take their own air supply. They carry tanks of air on their backs, and breathe it in through a mouthpiece. As the diver breathes out, you can see bubbles of stale air rising in the water.

LOOK AT ME! LOOK AT ME! LOOK AT ME! LOOK AT ME!

Have you ever tried snorkelling? You swim underwater and breathe through a tube, which reaches up to the air.

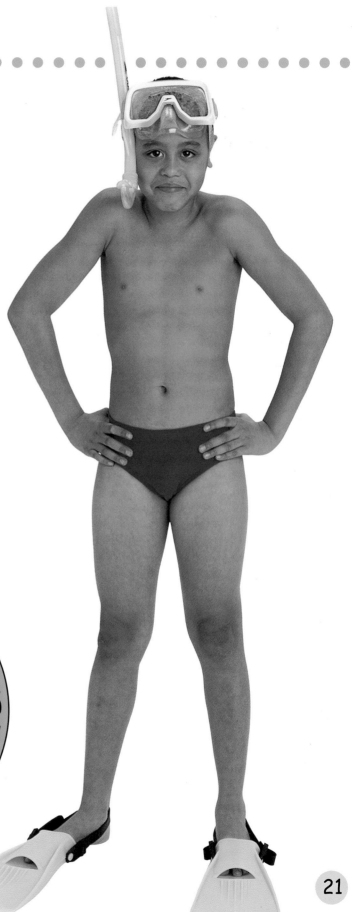

Healthy lungs

When you are born, your lungs are pale pink. But they get darker as you get older. This is because the dust, dirt and **germs** in the air you breathe make them dirty. Your body helps to keep your lungs clean. The inside of your nose is lined with tiny hairs and a slimy stuff, called **mucus**. Some dirt and germs stick to it as you breathe in air and you get rid of them when you blow your nose.

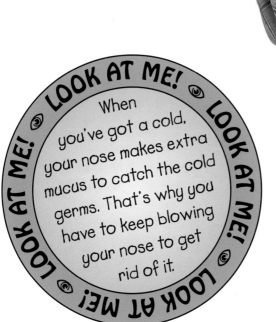

LOOK AT ME! LOOK AT ME! LOOK AT ME! LOOK AT ME!

When you've got a cold, your nose makes extra mucus to catch the cold germs. That's why you have to keep blowing your nose to get rid of it.

Your air tubes are also lined with mucus and covered in tiny hairs, too. These hairs are called **cilia**. The mucus and cilia catch dirt and germs, and push them away from your lungs.

When people smoke cigarettes, they breathe in harmful chemicals. These chemicals stop the cilia working, so dirt and mucus clog up the lungs. Smoking can cause serious illnesses, such as cancer and heart disease.

AMAZING!

Fumes from cars, factories and power stations add lots of dust and dirt to the air, too!

Cilia hairs in your air tubes, seen under a microscope.

Sneezes and coughs

If dust and germs get into your nose, sometimes you sneeze to get rid of them. Aaatchooo! When you sneeze, you take a sudden breath and shut off your nose and throat. Air builds up in your lungs, then your lungs suddenly shoot it out. This helps to clear your nose. When you sneeze, air blasts out of your nose at over 160 kilometres per hour. This is as fast as an express train!

AMAZING!

In summer, some people sneeze because of hay fever. This means that they are allergic to flower pollen!

24

Like sneezing, coughing helps to clear your air tubes. You can't stop yourself coughing or sneezing, it's automatic, just like breathing. But coughs and sneezes spread **diseases**. If you have a cold, the air you cough or sneeze out has millions of cold germs in it. If other people breathe in your germs, they may catch a cold too. That's why you should always catch a sneeze or a cough in a hanky.

LOOK AT ME! LOOK AT ME! LOOK AT ME! LOOK AT ME!

If you've got a bad cough, a spoonful of cough medicine can help your throat to feel better.

Speaking and singing

You use your air tubes for speaking and singing, too. Look in a mirror and swallow. Can you see a lump in your throat? This is your **voicebox**. Two thin strings of muscle lie across it, called your vocal cords. When you speak, air flows over them and makes them wobble. This wobbling makes the sound of your voice. Then your lips, teeth, tongue, nose and throat shape the sounds into words. Your voice can make some amazing sounds, from a quiet whisper to a very loud scream.

AMAZING!

The enormous blue whale has the loudest voice of any creature. It can sing twice as loudly as an opera singer!

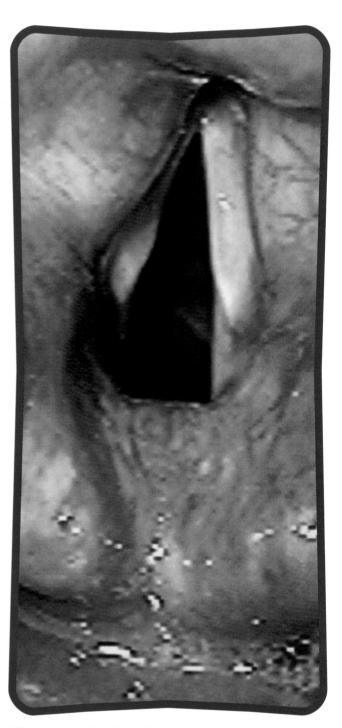

The vocal chords in your throat, seen under a microscope.

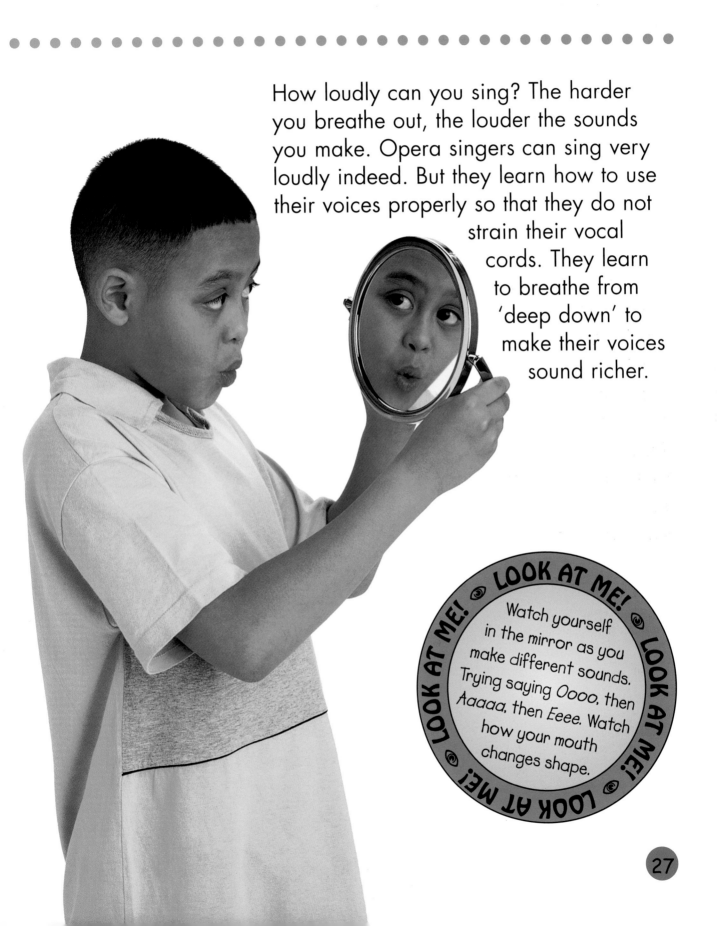

How loudly can you sing? The harder you breathe out, the louder the sounds you make. Opera singers can sing very loudly indeed. But they learn how to use their voices properly so that they do not strain their vocal cords. They learn to breathe from 'deep down' to make their voices sound richer.

LOOK AT ME! ◎ LOOK AT ME! ◎ LOOK AT ME! ◎ LOOK AT ME! ◎ LOOK AT ME!

Watch yourself in the mirror as you make different sounds. Trying saying Oooo, then Aaaaa, then Eeee. Watch how your mouth changes shape.

27

Glossary

Alveoli Tiny air bubbles in your lungs.

Blood vessels The thin tubes which carry blood around your body.

Bone marrow The jelly inside some of your bones. It makes new red blood cells.

Carbon dioxide A waste gas made in your body, which you have to breathe out.

Chest The top part of your body, below your neck, which contains your lungs.

Cilia Tiny hairs which line your air tubes. They are useful for trapping dust and germs.

Diaphragm A flat sheet of muscle under your lungs.

Diseases Another word for illnesses.

Energy Your body needs energy to make it work and move. You get energy from the food you eat.

Germs Tiny living things which cause some illnesses.

Mucus A slimy stuff which lines your nose, air tubes and lungs. It helps to protect them from germs.

Oxygen A gas in the air which you need to breathe to stay alive.

Respiratory system The parts of your body which you use for breathing. Respiration is the way in which your body uses the oxygen you breathe in to make it work. Carbon dioxide is the waste made by respiration. You breathe it out.

Voicebox The muscles in your throat, which help you to speak.

Index